Christian Perfection

Parts One & Two

Charles G Finney

ISBN 978-1-60386-765-8

DIGITALIZED BY
WATCHMAKER PUBLISHING

Christian Perfection

Part One

*Be ye therefore perfect, even as your
Father which is in heaven is perfect.* [1]

I n the 43rd verse, the Savior says, "Ye have heard that it hath been said, Thou shalt love thy neighbor, and hate thine enemy; but I say unto you, Love your enemies, bless them that curse you, do good to them that hate you, and pray for them which despitefully use you and persecute you; that ye may be the children of your Father which is in heaven: for He maketh his sun to rise on the evil and on the good, and sendeth rain on the just and on the unjust. For if ye love them which love you, what reward have ye? do not even the publicans the same? And if ye salute your brethren only, what do ye more than others? do not even the publicans so? Be ye therefore perfect, even as your Father which is in heaven is perfect."

In discoursing on the subject of Christian Perfection, it is my design to pursue this order:

I. I shall show what is not to be understood by this requirement, "Be ye therefore perfect;" or, what Christian Perfection is not.

II. Show what is the perfection here required.

III. That this perfection is a duty.

IV. That it is attainable; and,

V. Answer some of the objections which are commonly urged against the doctrine of Christian Perfection.

I. I am to show you what Christian Perfection is not.

1. It is not required that we should have the same natural perfections that God has.

God has two kinds of perfections, natural and moral. His natural perfections constitute his nature, essence, or constitution. They are his

---

[1] *Matthew v. 48 -*

eternity, immutability, omnipotence, &c. These are called natural perfections, because they have no moral character. They are not voluntary. God has not given them to himself, because he did not create himself, but existed from eternity, with all these natural attributes in full possession. All these God possesses in an infinite degree. These natural perfections are not the perfection here required. The attributes of our nature were created in us, and we are not required to produce any new natural attributes, nor would it be possible. We are not required to possess any of them in the degree that God possesses them.

2. The perfection required in the text is not perfection of knowledge, even according to our limited faculties.

3. Christian Perfection, as here required, is not freedom from temptation, either from our constitution or from things that are about us. The mind may be ever so sorely tried with the animal appetites, and yet not sin. The apostle James says, "Every man is tempted, when he is drawn away of his own lust, and enticed." The sin is not in the temptations, but in yielding to them. A person may be tempted by Satan, as well as by the appetites, or by the world, and yet not have sin. All sin consists in voluntarily consenting to the desires.

4. Neither does Christian perfection imply a freedom from what ought to be understood by the Christian warfare.

5. The perfection required is not the infinite moral perfection which God has; because man, being a finite creature, is not capable of infinite affections. God being infinite in himself, for him to be perfect is to be infinitely perfect. But this is not required of us.

II. I am to show what Christian perfection is; or what is the duty actually required in the text.

It is perfect obedience to the law of God. The law of God requires perfect, disinterested, impartial benevolence, love to God and love to our neighbor. It requires that we should be actuated by the same feeling, and to act on the same principles that God acts upon; to leave self out of the question as uniformly as he does, to be as much separated from selfishness as he is; in a word, to be in our measure as perfect as God is. Christianity requires that we should do neither more nor less than the law of God prescribes. Nothing short of this is Christian perfection. This is being, morally, just as perfect as God. Everything is here included, to feel as he feels, to love what he loves, and hate what he hates, and for the same reasons that he loves and hates.

God regards every being in the universe according to its real value. He regards his own interests according to their real value in the scale of being, and no more. He exercises the same love towards himself that he requires of us, and for the same reason. He loves himself supremely, both with the love of benevolence and the love of complacency, because he is supremely excellent. And he requires us to love him just so, to love him as perfectly as he loves himself. He loves himself with the love of benevolence, or regards his own interest, and glory, and happiness, as the supreme good, because it is the supreme good. And He requires us to love him in the same way. He loves himself with infinite complacency, because he knows that he is infinitely worthy and excellent, and he requires the same of us. He also loves his neighbor as himself, not in the same degree that he loves himself, but in the same proportion, according to their real value. From the highest angel to the smallest worm, he regards their happiness with perfect love, according to their worth. It is his duty to conform to these principles, as much as it is our duty. He can no more depart from this rule than we can, without committing sin; and for him to do it would be as much worse than for us to do it, as he is greater than we. God is infinitely obligated to do this. His very nature, not depending on his own volition, but uncreated, binds him to this. And he has created us moral beings in his own image, capable of conforming to the same rule with himself. This rule requires us to have the same character with him, to love as impartially, with as perfect love--to seek the good of others with as single an eye as he does. This, and nothing less than this, is Christian Perfection.

III. I am to show that Christian Perfection is a duty.

1. This is evident from the fact that God requires it, both under the law and under the gospel.

The command in the text, "Be ye perfect, even as your Father which is in heaven is perfect," is given under the gospel. Christ here commands the very same thing that the law requires. Some suppose that much less is required of us under the gospel, than was required under the law. It is true that the gospel does not require perfection, as the condition of salvation. But no part of the obligation of the law is discharged. The gospel holds those who are under it to the same holiness as those under the law.

2. I argue that Christian Perfection is a duty, because God has no right to require anything less.

God cannot discharge us from the obligation to be perfect, as I have defined perfection. If he were to attempt it, he would just so far give a license to sin. He has no right to give any such license. While we are moral beings, there is no power in the universe that can discharge us from the obligation to be perfect. Can God discharge us from the obligation to love Him with all our heart and soul and mind and strength? That would be saying that God does not deserve such love. And if he cannot discharge us from the whole law, he cannot discharge from any part of it, for the same reason.

3. Should any one contend that the gospel requires less holiness than the law, I would ask him to say just how much less it requires.

If we are allowed to stop short of perfect obedience, where shall we stop? How perfect are we required to be? Where will you find a rule in the Bible, to determine how much less holy you are allowed to be under the gospel, than you would be under the law? Shall we say each one must judge for himself? Then I ask, if you think it is your duty to be any more perfect than you are now? Probably all would say, Yes. Can you lay down any point at which, when you have arrived, you can say, "Now I am perfect enough; it is true, I have some sin left, but I have gone as far as it is my duty to go in this world?" Where do you get your authority for any such notion? No; the truth is, that all who are truly pious, the more pious they are, the more strongly they feel the obligation to be perfect, as God is perfect.

IV. I will now show that Christian Perfection is attainable, or practicable, in this life.

1. It may be fairly inferred that Christian Perfection is attainable, from the fact that it is commanded.

Does God command us to be perfect as he is perfect, and still shall we say it is an impossibility? Are we not always to infer, when God commands a thing, that there is a natural possibility of doing that which he commands? I recollect hearing an individual say, he would preach to sinners that they ought to repent, because God commands it; but he would not preach that they could repent, because God has nowhere said that they can. What consummate trifling! Suppose a man were to say he would preach to citizens, that they ought to obey the laws of the country because the government had enacted them, but he would not tell them that they could obey, because it is nowhere in the statute book enacted that they have the ability. It is always to be understood, when God requires anything of men, that they possess the requisite faculties to do it. Otherwise God requires of us impossibilities, on pain of death, and sends sinners to hell for not doing what they were in no sense able to do.

2. That there is natural ability to be perfect is a simple matter of fact.

There can be no question of this. What is perfection? It is to love the Lord our God with all our heart and soul and mind and strength and to love our neighbor as ourselves. That is, it requires us not to exert the powers of somebody else, but our own powers. The law itself goes no farther than to require the right use of the powers you possess. So that it is a simple matter of fact that you possess natural ability, or power, to be just as perfect as God requires.

OBJECTION. Here some may object, that if there is a natural ability to be perfect, there is a moral inability, which comes to the same thing, for inability is inability, call it what you will, and if we have moral inability, we are as really unable as if our inability was natural.

ANSWER 1. There is no more moral inability to be perfectly holy, than there is to be holy at all. So far as moral ability is concerned, you can as well be perfectly holy as you can be holy at all. The true distinction between natural ability and moral ability, is this: Natural ability relates to the powers and faculties of the mind; Moral ability only to the will. Moral inability is nothing else than unwillingness to do a thing. So it is explained by President Edwards, in his Treatise on the Will, and by other writers on the subject. When you ask whether you have moral ability to be perfect, if you mean by it, whether you are willing to be perfect, I answer, No. If you were willing to be perfect, you would be perfect; for the perfection required is only a perfect conformity of the will to God's law, or willing right. If you ask then, Are we able to will right? I answer, the question implies a contradiction, in supposing that there can be such a thing as a moral agent unable to choose, or will. President Edwards says expressly, in his chapter on Moral Inability, as you may see, if you will read it, that strictly speaking, there is no such thing as Moral

Inability. When we speak of inability to do a thing, if we mean to be understood, of a real inability, it implies a willingness to do it, but a want of power. To say, therefore, we are unable to will, is absurd. It is saying we will and yet are unable to will, at the same time.

ANSWER 2. But I admit and believe, that there is desperate unwillingness in the case. And if this is what you mean by Moral Inability, it is true. There is a pertinacious unwillingness in sinners to become Christians, and in Christians to become perfect, or to come up to the full perfection required both by the law and gospel. Sinners may strongly wish to become Christians, and Christians may strongly wish or desire to be rid of all their sins, and may pray for it, even with agony. They may think they are willing to be perfect, but they deceive themselves. They may feel, in regard to their sins taken all together, or in the abstract, as if they are willing to renounce them all. But take them up in the detail, one by one, and there are many sins they are unwilling to give up. They wrestle against sin in general, but cling to it in the detail.

I have known cases of this kind where individuals will break down in such a manner that they think they never will sin again; and then perhaps in one hour, something will come up that they are ready to fight for the indulgence, and need to be broken down again and again. Christians actually need to be hunted from one sin after another, in this way, before they are willing to give them up, and after all, are unwilling to give up all sins. When they are truly willing to give up all sin, when they have no will of their own, but merge their own will entirely in the will of God, then their bonds are broken. When they will yield absolutely to God's will, then they are filled with all the fulness of God.

After all, the true point of inquiry is this: Have I any right to expect to be perfect in this world? Is there any reason for me to believe that I can be so completely subdued, that my soul shall burn with a steady flame, and I shall love God wholly, up to what the law requires? That it is a real duty, no one can deny. But the great query is, Is it attainable?

I answer, Yes, I believe it is.

Here let me observe, that so much has been said within a few years about Christian Perfection, and individuals who have entertained the doctrine of Perfection have run into so many wild notions, that it seems as if the devil had anticipated the movements of the church, and created such a state of feeling, that the moment the doctrine of the Bible respecting the sanctification is crowded on the church, one and another cries out, "Why, this is Perfectionism." But I will say, notwithstanding the errors into which some of those called Perfectionists have fallen, there is such a thing held forth in the Bible as Christian Perfection, and that the Bible doctrine on the subject is what nobody need to fear, but what every body needs to know. I disclaim, entirely, the charge of maintaining the peculiarities, whatever they be, of modern Perfectionists. I have read their publications, and have had much knowledge of them as individuals, and I cannot assent to many of their views. But the doctrine that Christian Perfection is a duty, is one which I have always maintained, and I have been more convinced of it within a few months, that it is attainable in this life. Many doubt this, but I am persuaded it is true, on various grounds.

1. God wills it.

The first doubt which will arise in many minds, is this; "Does God really will my sanctification in this world?" I answer: He says he does. The law of God is itself as strong an expression as he can give of his will on the subject, and it is backed up by an infinite sanction. The gospel is but a republication of the same will, in another form. How can God express his will more strongly on this point than he has in the text? "Be ye therefore perfect, even as your Father which is in heaven is perfect." In the Thessalonians, iv. 3, we are told expressly, "For this is the will of God, even your sanctification." If you examine the Bible carefully, from one end to the other, you will find that it is everywhere just as plainly taught that God wills the sanctification of Christians in this world, as it is that he wills sinners should repent in this world. And if we go by the Bible, we might just as readily question whether he wills that men should repent, as whether he wills that Christians should be holy. Why should he not reasonably expect it? He requires it. What does he require? When he requires men to repent, he requires that they should love God with all the heart, soul, mind, and strength. What reason have we to believe that he wills they should repent at all, or love him at all, which is not a reason for believing that he wills they should love him perfectly? Strange logic, indeed! to teach that he wills it in one case, because he requires it, and not admit the same inference in the other. No man can show, from the Bible, that God does not require perfect sanctification in this world, nor that he does not will it, nor that it is not just as attainable as any degree of sanctification.

I have turned over the Bible with special reference to this point, and thought I would note down on my card, where I have the plan of my discourse, the passages that teach this doctrine. But I found they were altogether too numerous to do it, and that if I collected them all, I should do nothing else this evening, but stand and read passages of scripture. If you have never looked into the Bible with this view, you will be astonished to see how many more passages there are that speak of deliverance from the commission of sin, than there are that speak of deliverance from the punishment of sin. The passages that speak only of deliverance from punishment, are as nothing, in comparison of the others.

2. All the promises and prophecies of God, that respect the sanctification of believers in this world, are to be understood of course, of their perfect sanctification.

What is sanctification, but holiness? When a prophecy speaks of the sanctification of the church, are we to understand that it is to be sanctified only partially? When God requires holiness, are we to understand that of partial holiness? Surely not. By what principle, then, will you understand it of partial holiness when he promises holiness. We have been so long in the way of understanding the scriptures with reference to the existing state of things, that we lose sight of the real meaning. But if we look only at the language of the Bible, I defy any man to prove that the promises and prophecies of holiness mean anything short of perfect sanctification, unless the requirements of both the law and gospel are to be understood of partial obedience which is absurd.

3. Perfect sanctification is the great blessing promised, throughout the Bible.

The apostle says we have exceeding great and precious promises, and what are they, and what is their use? "Whereby are given unto us exceeding great and precious promises, that by these ye might be partakers of the divine nature, HAVING ESCAPED THE CORRUPTION that is in the world through lust." 2 Peter i.4. If that is not perfect sanctification, I beg to know what is. It is a plain declaration that these "exceeding great and precious promises" are given for this object, that by believing and appropriating and using them, we might become partakers of the divine nature. And if we will use them for the purposes for which they were put in the Bible, we may become perfectly holy.

Let us look at some of these promises in particular. I will begin with the promise of the Abrahamic covenant. The promise is that his posterity should possess the land of Canaan, and that through him, by the Messiah, all nations should be blessed. The seal of the covenant, circumcision, which everyone knows is a type of holiness, shows us what was the principal blessing intended. It was HOLINESS. So, the apostle tells us, in another place, Jesus Christ was given, that he might sanctify unto himself a peculiar people.

All the purifications and other ceremonies of the Mosaic ritual signified the same thing; as they are all pointed forward to a Savior to come. Those ordinances of purifying the body were set forth, every one of them, with reference to the purifying of the mind, or holiness.

Under the gospel, the same thing is signified by baptism; the washing of the body representing the sanctification of the mind.

In Ezekiel xxxvi. 25, this blessing is expressly promised, as the great blessing of the gospel: "Then will I sprinkle clean water upon you, and ye shall be clean: from all your filthiness, and from all your idols, will I cleanse you. A new heart also will I give you, and a new spirit will I put within you: and I will take away the stony heart out of your flesh, and I will give you a heart of flesh. And I will put my spirit within you: and cause you to walk in my statutes, and you shall keep my judgments, and do them."

So, it is in Jeremiah xxxiii. 8: "And I will cleanse them from all their iniquity, whereby they have sinned against me; and I will pardon all their iniquities, whereby they have sinned, and whereby they have transgressed against me." But it would take up too much time to quote all the passages in the Old Testament prophecies, that represent holiness to be the great blessing of the covenant. I desire you all to search the Bible for yourselves, and you will be astonished to find how uniformly the blessing of sanctification is held up as the principal blessing promised to the world through the Messiah.

Why, who can doubt that the great object of the Messiah's coming was to sanctify his people? Just after the fall it was predicted that Satan would bruise his heel, but that he should bruise Satan's head. And the apostle John tells us that "For this purpose the Son of God was manifested, that he might destroy the works of the devil." He has undertaken to put Satan under his feet. His object is to win us back to our allegiance to God, to sanctify us, to purify our minds. As it is said in Zech. xiii. 1, "In that day there shall be a fountain opened to the house of David and to the inhabitants of Jerusalem for sin and for uncleanness."

And Daniel says, "Seventy weeks are determined upon thy people and upon thy holy city, to finish the transgression, and to make an end of sins, and to make reconciliation for iniquity, and to bring in everlasting righteousness, and to seal up the vision and prophecy, and to anoint the Most Holy." But it is in vain to name the multitude of these texts. The Old Testament is full of it.

In the New Testament, the first account we have of the Savior, tells us, that he was called "JESUS, for he shall save his people from their sins." So, it is said, "He was manifested to take away our sins," and " to destroy the works of the devil." In Titus ii. 13, the apostle Paul speaks of the grace of God, or the gospel, as teaching us to deny ungodliness. "Looking for that blessed hope, and the glorious appearing of the great God, and our Savior Jesus Christ, who gave himself for us, that he might redeem us from all iniquity, and purify unto himself a peculiar people, zealous of good works." And in Ephesians v. 25, we learn that "Christ loved the church, and gave himself for it; that he might sanctify and cleanse it with the washing of water by the word, that he might present it to himself a glorious church, not having spot or wrinkle or any such thing; but that it should be holy and without blemish." I only quote these few passages by way of illustration, to show that the object for which Christ came is to sanctify the church to such a degree that it should be absolutely "holy and without blemish." So in Romans xi. 26, "And so all Israel shall be saved: as it is written, There shall come out of Sion the Deliverer, and shall turn away ungodliness from Jacob; For this is my covenant unto them, when I shall take away their sins." And in 1 John i. 9, it is said, "If we confess our sins, he is faithful and just to forgive us our sins, and to cleanse us from all unrighteousness." What is it to "cleanse us from ALL unrighteousness," if it is not perfect sanctification? I presume all of you who are here to-night, if there is such a thing promised in the Bible as perfect sanctification, wish to know it. Now, what do you think? In 1 Thessalonians, v. 23, the apostle Paul prays a very remarkable prayer: "And the very God of peace sanctify you wholly; and I pray God your whole spirit, and soul, and body, be preserved blameless unto the coming of our Lord Jesus Christ." What is that? "Sanctify you wholly." Does that mean perfect sanctification? You may think it does not mean perfect sanctification in this world. But the apostle says not only that your whole soul and spirit, but that your "body be preserved blameless." Could an inspired apostle make such a prayer, if he did not believe the blessing prayed for to be possible? But he goes on to say, in the very next verse, "Faithful is he that calleth you, who also WILL DO IT." Is that true, or is it false?

4. The perfect sanctification of believers is the very object for which the Holy Spirit is promised.

To quote the passages that show this, would take up too much time. The whole tenor of scripture respecting the Holy Spirit proves it. The whole array of gospel means through which the Holy Spirit works, is aimed at this, and adopted to the end of sanctifying the church. All the commands to be holy, all the promises, all the prophecies, all the ordinances, all the providences, the blessings and the judgments, all the duties of religion, are means which the Holy Ghost is to employ for sanctifying the church.

5. If it is not a practicable duty to be perfectly holy in this world, then it will follow that the devil has so completely accomplished his design in corrupting mankind, that Jesus Christ is at fault, and has no way to sanctify his people but by taking them out of the world.

Is it possible that Satan has so got the advantage of God, that God's kingdom cannot be re-established in this world, and that the Almighty has no way but to back out, and to take his saints to heaven, before he can make them holy? Is God's kingdom to be only partially established, and is it to be always so, that the best saints shall one-half of their time be serving the devil? Must the people of God always go drooping and driveling along in religion, and live in sin, until they get to heaven? What is that stone cut out of a mountain without hands, that is to fill the earth, if it does not show that there is yet to be a universal triumph of the love of God in the world?

6. If Perfect Sanctification is not attainable in this world, it must be, either from a want of motives in the gospel, or a want of sufficient power in the Spirit of God.

It is said that in another life we may be like God, for we shall see him as he is. But why not here, if we have that faith which is the "substance of things hoped for, and the evidence of things not seen?" There is a promise to those who "hunger and thirst after righteousness" that "they shall be filled." What is it to be "filled" with righteousness, but to be perfectly holy? And are we never to be filled with righteousness till we die? Are we to go through life hungry and thirsty and unsatisfied? So the Bible has been understood, but it does not read so.

OBJECTIONS.

1. "The power of habit is so great, that we ought not to expect to be perfectly sanctified in this life."

ANSWER. If the power of habit can be so far encroached upon that an impenitent sinner can be converted, why can it not be absolutely broken, so that a converted person may be wholly sanctified? The greatest difficulty, surely, is when selfishness has the entire control of the mind, and when the habits of sin are wholly unbroken. This obstacle is so great, in all cases, that no power but that of the Holy Ghost can overcome it, and so great in many instances, that God himself cannot, consistently with his wisdom, use the means necessary to convert the soul. But is it possible to suppose, that after he has begun to overcome it, after he has broken the power of selfishness and the obstinacy of habit, and actually converted the individual, that after this God has not resources sufficient to sanctify the soul altogether!

2. "Many physical difficulties have been created by a life of sin, that cannot be overcome or removed by moral means."

This is a common objection. Men feel that they have fastened upon themselves appetites and physical influences, which they do not believe it possible to overcome by moral means. The apostle Paul, in the 7th of Romans, describes a man in great conflict with the body. But in the next chapter he speaks of one who had gotten the victory over the flesh. "And if Christ be in you, the body is dead because of sin; but the spirit is life because of righteousness. But if the Spirit of him that raised up Jesus from the dead dwell in you, he that raised up Christ from the dead shall also quicken your mortal bodies by his Spirit that dwelleth in you." This quickening of the body is not spoken of the resurrection of the body, but of the influence of the Spirit of God upon the body--the sanctification of the body.

You will ask, "Does the Spirit of God produce a physical change in the body?" I will illustrate it by the case of the drunkard. The drunkard has brought upon himself a diseased state of the body, an unnatural thirst, which is insatiable, and so strong that it seems impossible he should be reclaimed. But very likely you know cases in which they have been reclaimed and have entirely overcome this physical appetite. I have heard of cases, where drunkards have been made to see the sin of drunkenness in such a strong light, that they abhorred strong drink, and forever renounced it, with such a loathing that they never had the least desire for strong drink again.

I once knew an individual who was a slave to the use of tobacco. At length he became convinced that it was a sin for him to use it, and the struggle against it finally drove him to God in such an agony of prayer, that he got the victory at once over the appetite, and never had the least desire for it again. I am not now giving you philosophy, but FACTS. I have heard of individuals over whom a life of sin had given to certain appetites a perfect mastery, but in time of revival they have been subdued into perfect quiescence, and these appetites have ever after been as dead as if they had no body. I suppose the fact is, that the mind may be so occupied and absorbed with greater things, as not to give a thought to the things that would revive the vicious appetite. If a drunkard goes by a grocery, or sees people drinking, and allows his mind to run upon it, the appetite will be awakened. The wise man, therefore, tells him to "Look not upon the wine when it is red." But there is no doubt that any appetite of the body may be subdued, if a sufficient impression is made upon the mind to break it up. I believe every real Christian will be ready to admit that this is possible, from his own experience. Have you not, beloved, known times when one great absorbing topic has so filled your mind, and controlled your soul, that the appetites of the body remained, for the time, perfectly neutralized? Now, suppose this state of mind to continue, to become constant; would not all these physical difficulties be overcome, which you speak of as standing in the way of perfect sanctification?

3. "The Bible is against this doctrine, where it says, there is not a just man on the earth, that liveth and sinneth not."

ANSWER. Suppose the Bible does say that there is not one on earth, it does not say there cannot be one. Or, it may have been true at that time, or under dispensation, that there was not one man in the world who was perfectly sanctified; and yet it may not follow that at this time, or under the gospel dispensation, there is no one who lives without sin. "For the law made nothing perfect, but the bringing in of a better hope did." Heb. 7. 9. i.e. The gospel did.

4. "The apostles admit that they were not perfect."

ANSWER. I know the apostle Paul says in one place, "Not as though I had already attained, either were already perfect." But it is not said that he continued so till his death, or that he never did attain to perfect sanctification, and the manner in which he speaks in the remainder of the verse, looks as if he expected to become so: "But I follow after, if that I may apprehend that for which also I am apprehended of Christ Jesus." Nor does it appear to me to be true that in this passage referred to, he is speaking of perfect sanctification, but rather of perfect knowledge.

And the apostle John speaks of himself as if he loved God perfectly. But whatever may be the truth, as to the actual character of the apostles, it does not follow, because they were not perfect that no others can be. They clearly declare it to be a duty, and that they were aiming at it, just as if they expected to attain it in this life. And they command us to do the same.

5. "But is it not presumption for us to think we can be better than the apostles and primitive Christians?"

ANSWER. What is the presumption in the case? Is it not a fact that we have far greater advantages for religious experience, than the primitive churches. The benefit of their experience, the complete scriptures, the state of the world, the near approach of the millennium, all give us the advantage over the primitive believers. Are we to suppose the church is always to stand in regard to religious experience, and never to go ahead in anything? What scripture is there for this? Why should not the church be always growing better? It seems to be the prevailing idea that the church is to be always looking back to the primitive saints as the standard. I suppose the reverse of this is a duty, and that we ought to be always aiming at a much higher standard than theirs. I believe the church must go far ahead of the primitive Christians, before the millennium can come. I leave out of view the apostles, because it does not clearly appear but what they become fully sanctified.

6. "But so many profess to be perfect, who are not so, that I cannot believe in perfection in this life."

ANSWER. How many people profess to be rich, who are not; Will you therefore say, you cannot believe anybody is rich? Fine logic!

7. "So many who profess perfection have run into error and fanaticism, that I am afraid to think of it."

ANSWER. I find in history, that a sect of Perfectionists has grown out of every great and general revival that ever took place. And this is exactly one of the devil's master-pieces, to counteract the effects of a revival. He knows that if the church were brought to the proper standard of holiness, it would be a speedy death blow to his power on earth, and he takes this course to defeat the efforts of the church for elevating the standard of piety, by frightening Christians from marching right up to the point, and aiming at living perfectly conformed to the will of God. And so successful has he been, that the moment you begin to crowd the church up to be holy, and give up all their sins, somebody will cry out, "Why, this leads to Perfectionism;" and thus give it a bad name and put it down.

8. "But do you really think anybody ever has been perfectly holy in this world?"

ANSWER. I have reason to believe there have been many. It is highly probable that Enoch and Elijah were free from sin, before they were taken out of the world. And in different ages of the church there have been numbers of Christians who were intelligent and upright, and had nothing that could be said against them, who have testified that they themselves lived free from sin. I know it is said, in reply, that they must have been proud, and that no man would say he was free from sin for any other motive but pride. But I ask, why may not a man say he is free from sin, if it is so, without being proud, as well as he can say he is converted without being proud? Will not the saints say it in heaven, to the praise of the grace of God, which has thus crowned his glorious work? And why may they not say it now, from the same motive? I do not myself profess now to have attained perfect sanctification, but if I had attained it, if I felt that God had really given me the victory over the world, the flesh and the devil, and made me free from sin, would I keep it a secret, locked up in my own breast, and let my brethren stumble on in ignorance of what the grace of God can do? Never. I would tell them, that they might expect complete deliverance, if they would only lay hold on the arm of help which Christ reaches forth, to save his people from their sins.

I have heard people talk like this, that if a Christian really was perfect, he would be the last person that would tell of it. But would you say of a person who professed conversion, "If he was really converted, he would be the last person to tell of it?" On the contrary, is it not the first impulse of a converted heart to say, "Come and hear, all ye that fear God, and I will declare what he hath done for my soul!" Why then should not the same desire exist in one who feels that he has obtained sanctification? Why all these suspicions, and refusing to credit evidence? If anyone gives evidence of great piety, if his life is irreproachable, and his spirit not to be complained of, if he shows the very spirit of the Son of God, and if such a person testifies that after great struggles and agonizing prayer God has given him the victory, and his soul is set at liberty by the power of divine grace; why are we not bound to receive his testimony, just as much, as when he says he is converted. We always take such testimony, so far. And now, when he says he has gone farther, and got the victory over all sin, and that Christ has actually fulfilled His promise in this respect, why should we not credit this also?

I have recently read Mr. Wesley's "Plain account of Christian Perfection," a book I never saw until lately. I find some expressions in it to which I should object, but I believe it is rather the expression than the sentiments. And I think, with this abatement, it is an admirable book, and I wish every member of this church would read it. An edition is in the press, in this city. I would also recommend the memoir of James Brainerd Taylor, and I wish every Christian would get it, and study it. I have read the most of it three times within a few months. From many things in that book, it is plain that he believed in the doctrine that Christian perfection is a duty, and that it is attainable by believers in this life. There is nothing published which shows that he professed to have attained it, but it is manifest that he believed it to be attainable. But I have been told that much which is found in his diary on this subject, as well as some things in his letters, were suppressed by his biographer, as not fitted for the eye of the church in her present state. I believe if the whole could come to light, that it would be seen that he was a firm believer in this doctrine. These books should be read and pondered by the church.

I have now in my mind an individual, who was a member of the church, but very worldly, and when a revival came he opposed it, at first; but afterwards he was awakened, and, after an awful conflict, he broke down, and has ever since lived a life of the most devoted piety, laboring and praying incessantly, like his blessed Master, to promote the kingdom of God. I have never heard this man say he thought he was perfect, but I have often heard him speak of the duty and practicability of being perfectly sanctified. And if there is a man in the world who is so, I believe he is one.

People have the strangest notions on this subject. Sometimes you will hear them argue against Christian Perfection on this ground, that a man who was perfectly holy could not live, could not exist in this world. I believe I have talked just so myself, in time past. I know I have talked like a fool on the subject. Why, a saint who was perfect would be more alive than ever, to the good of his fellow men. Could not Jesus Christ live on earth? He was perfectly holy. It is thought that if a person was perfectly sanctified, and loved God perfectly, he would be in such a state of excitement, that he could not remain in the body, could neither eat nor sleep, nor attend to the ordinary duties of life. But there is no evidence of this. The Lord Jesus Christ was a man, subject to all the temptations of other men. He also loved the Lord his God with all his heart and soul and strength. And yet it does not appear that he was in such a state of excitement that he could not both eat and sleep, and work at his trade as a carpenter, and maintain perfect health of body and perfect composure of mind. And why needs a saint that is perfectly sanctified, to be carried away with uncontrollable excitement, or killed with intense emotion, any more than Jesus Christ? There is no need of it, and Christian Perfection implies no such thing.

REMARKS

We can see now the reasons why there is no more perfection in the world.

1. Christians do not believe that it is the will of God, or that God is willing they should be perfectly sanctified in this world.

They know he commands them to be perfect, as he is perfect, but they think that he is secretly unwilling, and does not really wish them to be so; "Otherwise," say they, "why does he not do more for us, to make us perfect?" No doubt, God prefers their remaining as they are, to using any other means or system of influences to make them otherwise; because he sees that it would be a greater evil to introduce a new system of means than to let them remain as they are. Where one of the evils is unavoidable, he chooses the least of the two evils, and who can doubt that he prefers their being perfect in the circumstances in which they are, to their sinning in these circumstances. Sinners reason just as these professors reason. They say, "I don't believe he wills my repentance; if he did, he would make me repent." Sinner, God may prefer your continued impenitence, and your damnation, to using any other influences than he does use to make you repent. But for you to infer from this, that he does not wish you to yield to the influences he does use, is strange logic! Suppose your servant should reason so, and say, "I don't believe my master means I should obey him, because he doesn't stand by me all day, to keep me at work." Is that a just conclusion? Very likely, the master's time is so valuable, that it would be a greater evil to his business, than for that servant to stand still all day.

So, it is in the government of God. If God were to bring all the power of his government to bear on one individual, he might save that individual, while at the same time, it would so materially derange his government, that it would be a vastly greater evil than for that individual to go to hell. In the same way, in the case of a Christian, God has furnished him with all the means of sanctification, and required him to be perfect, and now he turns around and says, "God does not really prefer my being perfect; if he did, he would make me so." This is just the argument of the impenitent sinner, and no better in one case than the other. The plain truth is, God does desire, of both, that in the circumstances in which they are placed, they should do just what he commands them to do.

2. They do not expect it themselves.

The great part of the church does not really expect to be any more pious than they are.

3. Much of the time, they do not even desire perfect sanctification.

4. They are satisfied with their hunger and thirst after righteousness, and do not expect to be filled.

Here let me say, that hunger and thirst after holiness IS NOT HOLINESS. The desire of a thing is not the thing desired. If they hunger and thirst after holiness, they ought to give God no rest, till he comes up to his promise, that they shall be filled with holiness, or made perfectly holy.

5. They overlook the great design of the gospel.

Too long has the church been in the habit of thinking that the great design of the gospel is, to save men from the punishment of sin, whereas its real design and object is to deliver men FROM SIN. But Christians have taken the other ground and think of nothing but that they are to go on in sin, and all they hope for is to be forgiven, and when they die made holy in heaven. Oh, if they only realized that the whole frame-work of the gospel is designed to break the power of sin, and fill men on earth with all the fulness of God, how soon there would be one steady blaze of love in the hearts of God's people all over the world!

6. The promises are not understood, and not appropriated by faith.

If the church would read the Bible, and lay hold of every promise there, they would find them exceeding great and precious. But now the church loses its inheritance, and remains ignorant of the extent of the blessings she may receive. Had I time to-night, I could lead you to some promises which, if you would only get hold of and appropriate, you would know what I mean.

7. They seek it by the law, and not by faith.

How many are seeking sanctification by their own resolutions and works, their fastings and prayers, their endeavors and activity, instead of taking right hold of Christ, by faith, for sanctification, as they do for justification. It is all work, work, WORK, when it should be by faith in "Christ Jesus, who of God is made unto us wisdom, and righteousness, and SANCTIFICATION, and redemption." When they go and take right hold of the strength of God, they will be sanctified. Faith will bring Christ right into the soul, and fill it with the same spirit that breathes through himself. These dead works are nothing. It is faith that must sanctify, it is faith that purifies the heart, that faith which is the substance of things hoped for, takes hold of Christ and brings him into the soul, to dwell there the hope of glory; that the life which we live here should be by the faith of the Son of God. It is from not knowing, or not regarding this, that there is so little holiness in the church.

And finally,

8. From the want of the right kind of dependence.

Instead of taking scriptural views of their dependence and seeing where their strength is, and realizing how willing God is to give his Holy Spirit to them that ask, now and continually, and thus taking hold and holding on by the arm of God, they sit down, in unbelief and sin, to wait God's time, and call this depending on God. Alas, how little is felt, after all this talk about dependence on the Holy Spirit, how little is really felt of it, and how little is there of the giving up of the whole soul to his control and guidance, with faith in his power to enlighten, to lead, to sanctify, to kindle the affections, and fill the soul continually with all the fulness of God!

Christian Perfection

Part Two

Be ye therefore perfect, even as your Father
which is in heaven is perfect.

In speaking from these words, two weeks ago, I pursued the following order.

1. I showed what is implied in being perfect.
2. What Christian perfection is.
3. That it is a duty.
4. That it is attainable in this life.
5. Answered some objections, and then gave some reasons why so many persons are not perfect.

To-night my object is to mention some additional causes which prevent the great body of Christians from attaining perfect sanctification. As a matter of fact, we know that the church is not sanctified, and we ought to know the reasons. If the defect is in God, we ought to know it. If he has not provided a sufficient revelation, or if the power of the Holy Spirit is not adequate to sanctify his people in this world, we ought to understand it, so as not to perplex ourselves with idle endeavors after what is unattainable. And if the fault is in us, we ought to know it, and the true reasons ought to be understood, lest by any means we should charge God foolishly, even in thought, by imagining that he has required of us that which he has furnished us no adequate means of attaining.

I. The first general reason which I shall mention, for persons not being sanctified, is that they seek sanctification by works, and not by faith.

The religion of works assumes a great variety of forms; and it is interesting to see the ever-varying, shifting forms it takes:

1. One form is where men are aiming to live so as to render their damnation unjust. It matters not, in this case, whether they deem

themselves Christians or not, if they are in fact trying to live so as to render it unjust for God to send them to hell. This was the religion of the ancient Pharisees. And there are not a few, in the present day, whose religion is purely of this character. You will often find them out of the church, and perhaps ready to confess that they have never been born again. But yet they speak of their own works in a way that makes it manifest that they think themselves quite too good to be damned.

2. Another form of the religion of works is, where persons are not aiming so much to render it unjust in God to damn them, but are seeking by their works to recommend themselves to the mercy of God. They know they deserve to be damned and will forever deserve it. But they also know that God is merciful; and they think that if they live honest lives, and do many kind things to the poor, it will so recommend them to the general mercy of God, that he will not impute their iniquities to them, but will forgive their sins and save them. This is the religion of most modern moralists. Living under the gospel, they know they cannot be saved by their works, and yet they think that if they go to meeting, and help support the minister, and do this and that and the other kinds of good works, it will recommend them to God's mercy sufficiently for salvation. So far as I understand the system of religion held by modern Unitarians, this must be their system. Whether they understand it so, or admit it to be so, or not, as far as I can see, it comes to this. They set aside the atonement of Christ, and do not expect to be saved by the righteousness of Jesus Christ; and I know not on what they do depend, but this. They seem to have a kind of sentimental religion, and on this, with their morality and their liberality, they depend to recommend them to the mercy of God. On this ground they expect to receive the forgiveness of their sins, and to be saved.

3. Another form of the religion of works is, where persons are endeavoring to prepare themselves to accept of Christ.

They understand that salvation is only through Jesus Christ. They know that they cannot be saved by works, nor by the general mercy of God, without an atonement, and that the only way to be saved is by faith in Christ. But they have heard the relations of the experience of others, who went through a long process of distress before they submitted to Christ and found peace in believing. And they think a certain preparatory process is necessary, and that they must make a great many prayers and run hither and thither to attend meetings, and lie awake many nights, and suffer so much distress, and perhaps fall into despair, and then they shall be in a situation to accept of Christ. This is the situation of many convicted sinners. When they are awakened, and get so far as to find that they cannot be saved by their own works, then they set themselves to prepare to receive Christ. Perhaps some of you, who are here to-night, are in just this case. You dare not come to Christ just as you are, when you have made so few prayers, and attended so few meetings, and felt so little distress, and done so little and been so little engaged. And so, instead of going right to Christ for all you need, as a poor lost sinner, throwing yourself unreservedly into his hands, you set yourself to lash your mind into more conviction and distress, in order to prepare you to accept of Christ. Such cases are just about as common as convicted sinners are. How many there are, who abound in such works, and seem determined they will not fall down at once at the feet of Christ. It is not necessary to go into an argument here, to show that they are growing no better by all this process. There is no love to God in it, and no faith, and no religion. It is all mere mockery of God, and hypocrisy, and sin. There may be a great deal of feeling, but it is of no use; it brings them in fact no nearer to Christ; and after all, they have to do the very thing at last, which they might have done just as well at first.

Now suppose an individual should take it into his head that this is the way to become holy. Every Christian can see that it is very absurd, and that however he may multiply such works, he is not beginning to approach to holiness. The first act of holiness is to believe, to take hold of Christ by faith. And if a Christian, who is awakened to feel the need of sanctification, undertakes to go through a preparatory process of self-created distress, before he applies to Christ, it is just as absurd as for an awakened sinner to do it.

4. Another form of the religion of works is, where individuals perform works to beget faith and love.

The last mentioned class was where individuals are preparing to come to Christ. Here we suppose them to have come to Christ, and that they have accepted him, and are real Christians; but having backslidden they set themselves to perform many works to beget faith and love, or to beget and perfect a right state of feeling. This is one of the most common and most subtle forms in which the religion of works shows itself at the present day.

Now, this is very absurd. It is an attempt to produce holiness by sin. For if the feelings are not right, the act is sin. If the act does not proceed from faith and love, whatever they may do is sin. How idle, to think that a person, by multiplying sins, can beget holiness! And yet it is perfectly common for persons to think they can beget holiness by a course of conduct that is purely sinful. For certainly, any act that does not spring from love already existing, is sinful. The individual acts not from the impulse of faith that works by love and purifies the heart, but he acts without faith and love, with a design to beget those affections by such acts as these.

It is true, when faith and love exist, and are the propelling motive to action, the carrying of them out in action has a tendency to increase them. This arises from the known laws of mind, by which every power and every faculty gains strength by exercise. But the case supposed is where individuals have left their first love, if ever they had any, and then set themselves, without faith or love, to bustle about and warn sinners, or the like, under the idea that this is the way to wake up, or to become holy, or to get into the state of feeling that God requires. It is really most unphilosophical and absurd, and ruinous, to think of waking up faith in the soul, where it does not exist, by performing outward acts from some other motive. It is mocking God, to pretend, by doing things from wrong motives, to produce a holy frame of mind. By and by, I shall show where the deception lies, and how it comes to pass that any persons should ever dream of such a way of becoming sanctified. The fact is too plain to be proved, that pretending to serve God in such a way, so far from having any tendency to produce a right spirit, is in fact grieving the Holy Ghost, and insulting God.

So far as the philosophy of the thing is concerned, it is just like the conduct of convicted sinners. But there is one difference: the sinner, in spite of all his wickedness, may by and by learn his own helplessness, and actually renounce all his own works, and feel that his continued refusal to come to Christ, so far from being a preparation for coming, is only heaping up so many sins against God. But it is otherwise with those who think themselves to be already Christians, as I will explain by and by.

It is often remarked, by careful observers in religion, that many persons who abound in religious acts, are often the most hardened, and the farthest removed from spiritual feeling. If performing religious duties was the way to produce religious feeling, we should expect that ministers, and leaders in the church, would be always the most spiritual. But the fact is, that where faith and love are not in exercise, in proportion as persons abound in outward acts without the inward life, they become hardened and cold, and full of iniquity. They may have been converted but have backslidden, and so long as they are seeking sanctification in this way, by multiplying their religious duties, running around to protracted meetings, or warning sinners, without any spiritual life, they will never find it, but will in fact become more hardened and stupid. Or if they get into an excitement in this way, it is a spurious superficial state of mind that has nothing holy in it.

II. Another reason why so many persons are not sanctified is this: They do not receive Christ in all his relations, as he is offered in the gospel.

Most people are entirely mistaken here, and they will never go ahead in sanctification, until they learn that there is a radical error in the manner in which they attempt to attain it. Take a case: Suppose an individual who is convinced of sin. He sees that God might in justice send him to hell, and that he has no way in which he can make satisfaction. Now tell him of Christ's atonement, show him how Christ died to make satisfaction, so that God can be just and yet the justifier of them that believe in Jesus, he sees it to be right and sufficient, and exactly what he needs, and he throws himself upon Christ, in faith, for justification. He accepts him as his justification, and that is as far as he understands the gospel. He believes, and is justified, and feels the pardon of his sins. Now, here is the very attitude in which most convicted sinners stop. They take up with Christ in the character in which, as sinners, they most feel the need of a Savior, as the propitiation of their sins, to make atonement and procure forgiveness, and there they stop. And after that, it is often exceedingly difficult to get their attention to what Christ offers beyond. Say what you will in regard to Christ as the believer's wisdom and righteousness and his sanctification, and all his relations as a Savior from sin--they do not feel their need of him sufficiently to make them really throw themselves upon him in these relations. The converted person feels at peace with God, joy and gratitude fill his heart, he rejoices in having found a Savior that can stand between him and his Judge, he may have really submitted, and for a time, he follows on in the way of obedience to God's commandments. But, by and by, he finds the workings of sin in his members, unsubdued pride, his old temper breaking forth, and a multitude of enemies assaulting his soul, from within and without, and he is not prepared to meet them.

Hitherto, he has taken up Christ and regarded him, mainly, in one of his relations, that of a Savior to save him from hell. If I am not mistaken, the great mass of professing Christians lose sight, almost altogether, of many of the most interesting relations which Christ sustains to believers. Now, when the convert finds himself thus brought under the power of temptation, and drawn into sin, he needs to receive Christ in a new relation, to know more of the extent of his provision, to make a fresh application to him, and give a new impulse to his mind to resist temptation. This is not fully apprehended by many Christians. They never really view Christ, under his name Jesus, because he saves his people from their sins. They need to receive him AS A KING, to take the throne in their hearts, and rule over them with absolute and perfect control, bringing every faculty and every thought into subjection. The reason why the convert thus falls under the power of temptation, is that he has not submitted his own will to Christ, as a king, in everything, as perfectly as he ought, but is, after all, exercising his own self-will in some particulars.

Again: There are a multitude of what are called sins of ignorance, which need not be. Christians complain that they cannot understand the Bible, and there are many things concerning which they are always in doubt. Now, what they need is, to receive Christ as wisdom, to accept him in his relation as the source of light and knowledge. Who of you now attach a full and definite idea to the text which says, "We are in Christ Jesus, who of God is made unto us wisdom, and righteousness, and sanctification, and redemption?" What do you understand by it? It does not say he is a justifier, and a teacher, and a sanctifier, and a redeemer; but that he is wisdom, and righteousness, and sanctification, and redemption. What does that mean? Until Christians shall find out by experience, and know what that scripture meaneth, how can the church be sanctified? The church is now just like a branch plucked off from a vine; "Except ye abide in me, ye cannot bear fruit." Suppose a branch had power voluntarily to separate itself from the vine, and then should undertake to bring forth fruit, what would you think? So with the church; until Christians will go to the Eternal Source of sanctification, and wisdom, and redemption, it will never become holy. If they would become, by faith, absolutely united with him, in all those offices and relations in which he is offered, they would know what sanctification is.

I may, at some other time, take this text as the foundation of a separate discourse, and discuss these points, one by one, and show what this means. I will only say, at present, as much as this: that it means just what it says, and there is no need of explaining it away, as has too commonly been done. And when the church shall once take hold of Christ, in ALL his relations, as here set forth, they will know what it is, and will see that he is the light and the life of the world. To be sanctified by him, they must so embrace him, as to receive from him those supplies of grace and knowledge, which alone can purify the soul and give the complete victory over sin and Satan.

I will mention some reasons why Christians do not receive Christ in all his relations.

(1.) They may not have those particular convictions, that are calculated to make them deeply feel the necessity of a Savior in those relations.

If an individual is not deeply convicted of his own depravity, and has not learned intimately his own sinfulness, and if he does not know experimentally, as a matter of fact, that he needs help to overcome the power of sin, he will never receive Jesus Christ into his soul AS A KING. When men undertake to help themselves out of sin, and feel strong in their own strength to cope with their spiritual enemies, they never receive Christ fully, nor rely on him solely to save them from sin. But when they have tried to keep themselves by their own watchfulness and prayers, and binding themselves by resolutions and oaths to obey God, and find that, after all, if left to themselves, there is nothing in them but depravity, then they feel their own helplessness, and begin to inquire what they shall do? The Bible teaches all this plainly enough, and if people would believe the Bible, converts would know their own helplessness, and their need of a Savior to save from sin, at the outset. But, as a matter of fact, they do not receive nor believe the Bible on this subject, until they have set themselves to work out a righteousness of their own, and thus have found out by experiment that they are nothing without Christ. And therefore, they do not receive him in this relation, till after they have spent, it may be, years, in these vain and self-righteous endeavors to do the work of sanctification themselves. Having begun in the spirit they are trying to be made perfect by the flesh.

(2.) Others, when they see their own condition, do not receive Christ as a Savior from sin, because they are, after all unwilling to abandon all sin.

They know that if they give themselves up entirely to Christ, all sin must be abandoned; and they have some idol which they are unwilling to give up.

(3.) Sometimes, when persons are deeply convinced, and anxious to know what they shall do to get rid of sin, they do not apply to Christ in faith, because they do not know what they have a right to expect from him.

There are many who seem to suppose they are under a fatal necessity to sin, and that there is no help for it, but they must drag along this load of sin till their death. They do not absolutely charge God foolishly, and say in words that he has made no provision for such a case as this. But they seem to suppose that Christ's atonement being so great as to cover all sins, and God's mercy being so great, if they do go on in sin all their days, as they expect they shall, he will forgive all at last, and it will be just about as well in the end, as if they had been really sanctified. They do not see that the gospel has made provision sufficient to rid us forever of the commission of all sin. They look at it as merely a system of pardon, leaving the sinner to drag along his load of sin to the very gate of heaven; instead of a system to break up the very power of sin in the mind. The consequence is, they make very little account of the promises. O, how little use do Christians make of those exceeding great and precious promises, in the Bible, which were given expressly for this purpose, that we might become partakers of the divine nature! Here God has suited his promises to our exigencies, for this end, and we have only to draw upon him for all that we want, and we shall have whatever we need for our sanctification. Hear the Savior say, "What things soever ye desire when ye pray, BELIEVE that ye receive them and ye shall have them."

The fact is, Christians do not really believe much that is in the Bible. Now, suppose you were to meet God, and you knew it was God himself, speaking to you, and he should reach out a book in his hand, and tell you to take that book, and that the book contains exceeding great and precious promises, of all that you need, or ever can need, to resist temptation, to overcome sin, and to make you perfectly holy, and fit you for heaven; and then he tells you that whenever you are in want of anything for this end, you need only take the appropriate promise, and present it to him at any time, and he will do it. Now, if you were to receive such a book, directly from the hand of God, and knew that God had written it for you, with his own hand, would you not believe it? And would you not read it a great deal more than you now read the Bible? How eager you would be to know all that was in it? And how ready to apply the promises in time of need! You would want to get it all by heart, and often repeat it all through, that you might keep your mind familiar with its contents, and be always ready to apply the promises you read! Now, the truth is, the Bible is that book. It is written just so, and filled with just such promises; so that the Christian, by laying hold of the right promise, and pleading it, can always find all that he needs for his spiritual benefit.

Christ is a complete Savior. All the promises of God are in him Yea, and in him Amen, to the glory of God the Father. That is, God has promised in the second person of the Trinity, in the person of Jesus Christ, and made them all certain through him. Now, the thing which is needed is, that Christians should understand these promises, and believe them, and in every circumstance of need apply them, for sanctification. Suppose they lack wisdom. Let them go to God, and plead the promise. Suppose they cannot understand the scriptures, or the path of duty is not plain. The promise is plain enough, take that. Whatever they lack of wisdom, righteousness, sanctification, and redemption, only let them go to God in faith, and take hold of the promise, and if he does not prove false, they will assuredly receive all that they need.

(4.) Another reason why many do not receive Christ in all his relations, is that they are too proud to relinquish all self-dependence or reliance on their own wisdom and their own will.

How great a thing it is, for the proud heart of man to give up its own wisdom, and knowledge, and will, and every thing, to God! I have found this the greatest of all difficulties. Doubtless all find it so. The common plea is, "Our reason was given us, to be exercised in religion, but what is the use, if we may not rely on it, or follow it?" But there is one important discrimination to be made, which many overlook. Our reason was given us to use in religion; but it is not in the proper province of reason to ask whether what God says is reasonable, but to show us the infinite reasonableness of believing that ALL which God says must be true, whether we in our ignorance and blindness can see the reasonableness of it or not. And if we go beyond this, we go beyond the proper province of reason. But how unwilling the proud heart of man is to lay aside all its own vain wisdom, and become like a little child, under the teaching of God! The apostle says, "If any man think that he knoweth anything, he knoweth nothing yet as he ought to know." There is a vast meaning in this. He that does not receive Christ alone as his wisdom, knows nothing in religion to any purpose. If he is not taught by Jesus Christ, he has not learned the first lesson of Christianity. So again, "No man knoweth the Father but the Son, and he to whomsoever the Son revealeth him." The individual who has learned this lesson, feels that he has not one iota of knowledge in religion, that is of any value, only as he is taught by Jesus Christ. For it is written, "And they shall all be taught of God."

REMARKS

I. You see what kind of preaching the church now needs.

The church needs to be searched thoroughly, shown their great defects, and brought under conviction, and then pointed to where their great strength lies. With their everlasting parade of dead works, they need to be shown how poor they are. "Thou sayest I am rich, and increased with goods, and have need of nothing, and knowest not that thou art wretched, and miserable, and poor, and blind, and naked." Until Christians are shown their poverty, and the infinite emptiness and abominable wickedness of their dead works, and then shown just where their help is, and that it is by FAITH ALONE they can never be sanctified, the church will go farther and farther from God, till it will have only the form of godliness, denying the power thereof.

II. When you see the Christian character defective in any particular, you may always know that the individual needs to receive Christ more fully in the very relation that is calculated to supply this defect.

The defect, whatever it be, in the character of any believer, will never be remedied, until he sees the relation of Christ to that part of his character, so as by faith to take hold of Christ and bring him in to remedy that defect. Suppose a person is naturally penurious and selfish, and reluctant to act in a disinterested manner; he will never remedy that defect, until he receives Christ as his pattern, and the selfishness is driven out of his heart by imbuing his very soul with the infinite benevolence of the Savior. So, it is with regard to any other defect; he will never conquer it, until you make him see that the infinite fulness of Christ is answerable to that very want.

III. You see the necessity there is that ministers should be persons of deep experience in religion.

It is easy for even a carnal mind to preach so as to bring sinners under conviction. But until the tone of sanctification is greatly raised among ministers, it is not to be expected that the piety of the church will be greatly elevated. Those Christians who have experience of these things should therefore be much in prayer for ministers, that the sons of Levi may be purified, that the leaders of Israel may take hold of Christ for the sanctification of their own hearts, and then they will know what to say to the church on the subject of holiness.

IV. Many seek sanctification by works, who do not know that they are seeking in this way.

They profess that they are seeking sanctification only by faith. They tell you they know very well that it is in vain to seek it in their own strength. But yet the results show how conclusively, that they are seeking by works, and not by faith. It is of the last importance that you should know, whether you are seeking sanctification by works, or by faith, for all seeking of it by works is absurd, and never will lead to any good results. How will you know?

Take again the case of a convicted sinner. Sinner, how are you seeking salvation? The sinner replies, "By faith, of course; everybody knows that no sinner can be saved by works." I say, No, you are seeking salvation by works. How shall I show it to him? Sinner, do you believe in Christ? "I do." But does he give you peace with God? "O no, not yet, but I am trying to get more conviction, and to pray more, and be more earnest in seeking, and I hope he will give me peace if I persevere." Now, every Christian sees, at a glance, that with all his pretensions to the contrary, this man is seeking salvation by works. And the way to prove it to him is exceedingly simple. It is evident he is seeking by works, because he is relying on certain preparatory steps and processes to be gone through, before he exercises saving faith. He is not ready now to accept of Christ, he is conscious he is not, but thinks he must bring himself into a different state of mind as a preparation, and it is at this he is aiming. That is works. No matter what the state of mind is, that he aims at as preparatory to coming to Christ; if it is anything that must precede faith, or any preparatory process for faith, and he is trying without faith to get into a proper state of mind to have faith, it is all the religion of works.

Now, how common is just such a state of mind among those Christians who profess to be seeking sanctification. You say, you must mortify sin, but the way you go about it is by a self-righteous preparation, seeking to recommend yourselves to Christ as worthy to receive the blessing, instead of coming right to Christ, as an unworthy and ruined beggar, to receive at once, by faith, the very blessing you need. No efforts of your own are going to make you any better. Like a person in a horrible pit of miry clay, every struggle of your own sinks you deeper in the clay. You have no need of any such thing, and all your endeavors, instead of bringing you any nearer to Christ, are only sinking you down in the filth, farther and farther from God. It is not even the beginning of help.

The sinner, by his preparatory seeking, gains no advantage. There he lies, dead in trespasses and sins, as far removed from spiritual life, or holiness, as ever a dead corpse was from natural life; until at length, ceasing from his own dead works, he comes to the conviction that there is nothing he can do for himself but to go NOW, just as he is, and submit to Christ. As long as he thinks there is something he must do first, he never feels that now is God's time of salvation. And as long as the Christian is seeking sanctification in the way of works, he never feels that now is God's time to give him the victory over sin.

V. Multitudes deceive themselves in this matter, by the manner in which they have seen certain old-fashioned, Antinomian churches roused up, who were dragging along in death.

Where such a church has been found, that had been fed on dry doctrine till they were about as stupid as the seats they sat on, the first thing has been to rouse them up to do something, and that very fact perhaps would bring such a church under conviction, and lead them to repentance. It is not because there is any religion in these doings of professors in such a state; but it shows them their deficiencies, and their unfitness to be members of the church, and awakens their consciences. So it is, sometimes, when a careless sinner has been set to praying. Everybody knows there is no piety in such prayers, but it calls his attention to the subject of religion, and gives the Holy Spirit an opportunity to bring the truth full upon his conscience. But if you take a man who has been in the habit of praying from his childhood, and whose formal prayers have made him as cold as a stone, praying will never bring that man under conviction, till you show him what is the true character of his prayers, and STOP his ungodly and heaven-daring praying.

In many cases, where a church has sunk down in stupidity, the most effectual way to rouse them has been found to be, setting them to warning sinners of their danger. This would get the attention of the church to the subject of religion, and perhaps bring many of them to repentance. Hence many have formed a general rule, that the way for a church to wake up, always is, to go to work, and warn sinners. They do not discriminate, here, between the habits of different churches, and the different treatment they consequently require. Whereas, if you take what is called a "working church," where they have been in the habit of enjoying revivals and holding protracted meetings, you will find there is no difficulty in rousing up the church to act, and bustle about, and make a noise. But as a general rule, unless there is great wisdom and faithfulness in dealing with the church, every succeeding revival will make their religion more and more superficial; and their minds will be more hardened instead of being convicted, by their efforts. Tell such a church they are self-righteous, and that there is no Holy Ghost in their bustling, and they will be affronted and stare at you, "Why, don't you know that the way to wake up in religion is to go to work in religion?" Whereas, the very fact that activity has become a habit with them, shows that they require a different course. They need first to be thoroughly probed and searched, and made sensible of their deficiencies, and brought humble and believing to the foot of the cross, for sanctification.

When I was an evangelist, I labored in a church that had enjoyed many revivals, and it was the easiest thing in the world to get the church to go out and bring in sinners to the meetings; and the impenitent would come in and hear, but there was no deep feeling, and no faith in the church. The minister saw that this way of proceeding was ruining the church, and that each successive revival, brought about in this manner, made the converts more and more superficial, and unless we came to a stand, and got more sanctification in the church, we should defeat our object. We began to preach with that view, and the church members writhed under it. The preaching ran so directly across all their former notions, about the way to promote religion, that some of them were quite angry. They would run about, and talk, but would do nothing else. But after a terrible state of things many of them broke down, and became as humble and as teachable as little children.

Now there are multitudes in the churches who insist upon it that the way to get sanctification is to go to work, and they think that, by dint of mere friction, they can produce the warm love of God in their hearts. This is all wrong. Mere driving about and bustle and noise will never produce sanctification. And least of all, when persons have been accustomed to this course.

VI. You that are in the habit of performing many religious duties, and yet fall short of holiness, can see what is the matter.

The truth is, you have gone to work to wake up, instead of at once throwing yourself on the Lord Jesus Christ for sanctification, and then going to work to serve him. You have gone to work for your life instead of working from a principle of life within, impelling you to the work of the Lord. You have undertaken to get holiness by a lengthened process, like that of the convicted sinner, who is preparing to come to Christ. But the misfortune is, that you have not half the perseverance of the sinner. The sinner is driven by the fear of going to hell, and he exerts himself in the way of works till his strength is all exhausted, and all his self-righteousness is worked up, and then, feeling that he is helpless and undone, he throws himself into the arms of Christ. But you have not so much perseverance, because you have not so much fear. You think you are a Christian, and that however you may come short of sanctification, yet you are safe from hell, and can go to heaven without it. And so, you will not persevere and put forth your efforts for holiness by works, till you have used up all your self-righteousness, and are driven to Christ as your only hope for sanctification. This is the reason why convicted Christians so generally fall short of that submission to Christ for holiness, which the convicted sinner exercises for forgiveness.

You say to the sinner, who is seeking salvation by works, "Why don't you yield up all your self-righteous efforts, and come right to Christ for salvation? He is ready to receive you NOW!" And why don't you do so too? When will you learn the first lesson in religion, that you have no help in yourselves, and that all your exertions without Christ, for sanctification, are just as vain as it is for the wretch who is in the horrible pit and miry clay, by his own struggling to get himself out.

VII. The growth of works in the church is no certain sign of growth in holiness.

If the church grows in holiness, it will grow in works. But it does not follow, that growth in works always proves growth in holiness. It may be that works of religion may greatly increase, while the power of religion is actually and rapidly declining. It often happens in a church, that when a revival begins to lose its power, the church may be willing to do even more than ever, in works, but it will not arrest the decline, unless they get broken down before God.

I see I must take up this subject again. O, that I could convince the whole church that they need no other help but Christ, and that they would come at once to Christ for all they want, and receive him as their wisdom, and righteousness, and sanctification, and redemption. How soon would all their wants be supplied, from his infinite fulness.

www.ingramcontent.com/pod-product-compliance
Lightning Source LLC
Chambersburg PA
CBHW020446030426
42337CB00014B/1413